How You Are Changing

A Guide for the Christian Family

For *boys* ages 9–11

For Discussion or Individual Use
Book 3 of the Learning about Sex Series for Boys
The Titles in the Series:

Book 1: Why Boys and Girls Are Different

Book 2: Where Do Babies Come From?

Book 3: How You Are Changing

Book 4: Sex and the New You

Book 5: Love, Sex, and God

Book 6: How to Talk Confidently with Your Child about Sex

Acknowledgments

We wish to thank all medical, child development, and family
life consultants who have assisted in the development, updating, and
revising of the Learning about Sex series.

Copyright © 1982, 1988, 1995, 1998, 2008, 2015 Concordia Publishing House
3558 S. Jefferson Ave., St. Louis, MO 63118-3968
1-800-325-3040 • www.cph.org

From text originally written by Jane Graver
Unless otherwise noted internal illustrations and photographs
© iStock.com.

Manufactured in East Peoria, IL/063692/416283

7 8 9 10 11 12 13 14 15 16   30 29 28 27 26 25 24 23 22

CONTENTS

Foreword

This book is one in a series of six designed to help parents communicate biblical values to their children in the area of sexuality. *How You Are Changing* is the third book in the series. It is written especially for boys ages 9 to 11 and, of course, for the parents, teachers, and other concerned grown-ups who may want to discuss the book with the children in their care. (See "A Note to Parents" on page 6 for ways to use the book and ways to communicate Christian values about sex in the home.)

Like its predecessor, the updated Learning about Sex series provides information about the mental, emotional, physical, and spiritual aspects of human sexuality. Moreover, it does so from a distinctively Christian point of view, in the context of our relationship to the God who created us and redeemed us in Jesus Christ. The series presents sex as another good gift from God and helps us understand it in the larger context of our entire life of faith. To counter cultural influences, be strong and consistent in communicating the miracle of God's design. The way God made us is just the way He knew it should be for our health and happiness.

Each book in the series is graded—in vocabulary and in the amount of information it provides. It answers the questions that children at each age level typically ask. Because children vary widely in their growth rates and interest levels, parents and other concerned adults will want to preview each book in the series, directing each child to the next graded book when he is ready for it.

In addition to reading the books, parents can use them as starting points for casual conversation and when answering other questions children might have. We pray that this will be the beginning of ongoing, open, honest, and intentional communication with your child regarding God's magnificent design.

The books in this series also can be used as mini units or as part of another course of study in a Christian school or church setting. Whenever the books are used in a class setting, it is important to let the parents know beforehand, since they have the primary responsibility for the education of their children. If used in a classroom setting, the books in this series are designed for separate single-gender groups, the setting most conducive to open conversations about questions and concerns. As the Christian home and the Christian school and church work together, Christian values in sex education can be more effectively strengthened.

The Editors

5

A Note to Parents

Is all this factual information really necessary for nine- to eleven-year-olds? It's probably a lot more than we knew when we were that age. Our children are living in a different world than the one in which we grew up. They are exposed to distorted information about sex every day—through TV shows, movies, the Internet, the words to popular music, and from their friends at school (Christian schools too). If they already have a solid foundation of knowledge and attitudes, they can evaluate the improper values and the misinformation they get from other sources instead of accepting whatever they hear or learning only as a reaction to a negative situation.

Research has shown that children are far more likely to develop healthy attitudes about their sexuality when parents encourage discussions about sex. Too much information does not seem to do any harm when linked to positive values. The child who feels unable to ask questions is far more likely to become preoccupied with sex than the one who has open access to information.

Of course, boys ages 9–11 will vary widely in their ability to understand the material in this book. You are the best judge of what is appropriate for your own child at each stage of his development. To decide whether this book is too advanced or too easy for your son, examine the books in this series that come immediately before and after this one.

How should you use this book? We recommend that you either read it with your son or let him read it and then discuss sections about which he has questions. Most children will not want to read all of it at once. They will probably be interested in different sections at different stages of their development. Another option is to use the book as a "what to say" resource as you talk with your son.

Ideally, this book will be used as part of a biblically based, broadly focused—yet personal—training program to prepare young boys for manhood. For young men, this training can flow from a mentoring relationship similar to that of Paul and Timothy. A young man can learn much from a father, grandfather, or other adult who trusts in Jesus for his salvation.

In the context of such a relationship, questions of a personal nature can be asked and answered, insightful discussions held, and godly behaviors modeled. Your expression of positive and God-pleasing values will likely have a greater

impact on the healthy development of your son than any book, other than the Bible. God's plan unfolds as each generation in succession passes on the truths God imparts through His Word and the wisdom that comes as challenges are met and overcome by the power of God's grace through Jesus.

Why do we suggest that sex education begin at an early age? Nearly all the young adults we questioned about their memory of the sex education they had in their own homes said something like "too little, too late. It turned me off to have to listen to a bunch of stuff I already knew—or thought I knew."

Where did these parents go wrong? Perhaps they were waiting for questions, but no questions came. Did that mean their child wasn't interested? Of course not. Perhaps the child had sensed his parents' discomfort. Or maybe he had learned that sex is a subject some people prefer not to discuss.

What if talking about sex is difficult for you? It is important to teach our children that sex is far more than what we "do" with our bodies. Sex is about who we are as people of God. If we help our children to have a healthy identity as a boy or a girl, then our children can begin to see sexual behavior as just one part of God's design for them as male and female. Talk about the unique and wonderful differences of boys and girls with your children. You can tell your child about your feelings, about how you appreciate and value how God made you. You can acknowledge that talking about body changes and the act of sex is difficult because you see your little children growing into adult men and women.

You may also say, "This is so special, so private, but I'm excited to talk about it with you, even if it seems awkward. Thank you for asking such a good question; that really helps." You will find that once trust and openness are established, it will be easier for everyone.

Your child will learn better and remember more from a series of shorter conversations than from a long, serious talk that may be put off because of the difficulty of finding the right time and place for it. Be ready for some surprises. When you show your child that it's okay to talk about sex, he'll ask questions whenever and wherever he happens to think of them.

Many young people who criticized their parents as sex educators admitted that the parents' attitudes and values came through, in spite of their clumsiness in expressing them. It's comforting to know that we can make mistakes without necessarily ruining our children, isn't it? Somehow, God blesses our bumbling efforts and makes them work far better than we would have dreamed possible.

What's the main point to emphasize in your talks? Communicate not only accurate information about the way God made us male or female, but especially a sense of wonder and deep appreciation of the beauty of God's marvelous design and purpose a well as a sense of respect and responsibility toward all God has given.

How to Use This Book

1. You can sit down and read all of the book at once, or you can use the contents section to look up questions you may have. It's a good idea to talk over what you learn with an adult you can trust and to pray about your discussions.

2. Some pages have pictures with labels on them. Be sure to study the pictures and read the labels very carefully.

3. "Some Words Used in This Book" (see page 69) can help you understand and pronounce the technical words you'll find in this book.

You Are Wonderful 1

God thinks you're special. You're His child. He knows you better than you know yourself. God carefully, lovingly designed you.

He made you different from every other kid in the whole world. In fact, you are different from every other kid who has ever lived! Your fingerprints, footprints, and eyes are different from those of any other person. Nobody else has your special mix of hair color, freckles, talents, likes and dislikes, and the million other things that make you *you*. When God made you, He made you one of a kind. You came from your mother and father, but it is God who gave you life and blessed them with you.

God knows you. He knows everything about you. And *God loves you just as you are*. That's not the same as loving everything you do.

We are all human beings and sinners. Sadly, we know that sin has been part of our human nature ever since sin first entered the world. Sin didn't change God's love for us, but it did change how we understand ourselves. The world wants you to think you're not smart enough, not handsome enough, not likable enough, not athletic enough . . . the list goes on. Your sinful flesh tempts you into making bad choices with bad consequences. The devil wants your relationships with your friends and family to be full of hurt.

But God gives new life through Jesus, and *you can see yourself as God sees you. You are a child of God.* Because of sin, the only thing you deserve is eternal death. But because you are a child of God, God loved you enough to send His Son, Jesus, to be your Savior. He loves you so much that He wants to be with you forever. So because of Jesus, you have eternal life in heaven. God doesn't see your sin. And because you are a child of God, the Holy Spirit strengthens you each day so the devil, the world, and our sinful flesh no longer has control of you. A child of God with Christ in you . . . that's who you are.

God created people to be male or female. Male and female are the words we use to describe a person's **sex**. Your sex—your male or female body design—is a very important gift from God. He made you that way for a reason, on purpose. Because you are a male, you can be a father someday. What other differences are there between being a male and a female? The differences are not just related to appearance.

Our brains are wired differently so males and females don't look at and process things the same way. Pediatric nurses in hospitals often note that even newborn babies already indicate distinctiveness, with baby girls tending to focus eye contact on a person, while baby boys seem to look all over to take in the big picture.

And not only has God made males and females different biologically (physically), but our culture and society views things as **feminine** or **masculine**. In that way, our sex is also called our **gender**. How wonderful it is to have two similar but very unique and distinct sexes as part of humanity!

That's the way God wanted it to be. These differences do not mean that one sex is better than the other. They just mean that God made male and female with gender (sex)-related characteristics we can celebrate and thank God for.

Males and females need one another and are a blessing to one another. God's view of male and female is not of a difference that competes, separates, or conflicts. Rather it is God-pleasing when our unique abilities and perspectives support and complement each other. 1 Corinthians 11:11 says, "In the Lord woman is not independent of man nor man of woman." Key words that describe a God-pleasing male/female relationship include respect, encouragement, cooperation, sharing, and caring.

Some people may say that boys and girls are the same, but there are important differences that are designed and intended by God that we cannot ignore. There are many ways that all people are alike, but these are factors that relate to being a human rather than being a male or female. One way we are all the same is that we are loved by God and saved through faith in Jesus. Galatians 3:28 says, "There is neither Jew nor Greek, there is neither slave nor free, there is no male and female, for you are all one in Christ Jesus." This does not say we are the same. It says that though each is distinct, one is not better than the other. All who are in Christ have equal standing before God and an equal share of the inheritance in heaven He has obtained for us. We are all special, loved, important children of God.

Your Emotions Are Important

An emotion is a strong feeling, such as love, anger, joy, hate, excitement, or fear. ***Emotions are a part of your body and who you are***; they are connected to your biological system (and affected by your own personal set of experiences). Research shows that **hormones** (a chemical substance produced by your body) are linked to a person's emotional well-being.

Emotions are usually in reaction toward something and usually involve a physical response (reaction) in your body. For example, if you're walking on the road and you see a car coming toward you, your body changes involuntarily (e.g., your pulse races) and then you decide what your (voluntary) reaction will be (e.g., you might jump out of the way).

You have **feelings** when your body is aware of that emotional state or reaction. For example, you may feel happy for a long time after an initial, short-term feeling (emotional response) of joy after something good happens to you.

Know that it is normal for a person to cry when he feels sad. (Even Jesus cried. Read about it in John 11:32–35.) Both males and females—all humans—cry. That's how God made us. People who try to be too tough to cry often become unable to show any feelings—love and joy as well as sadness. The bottled-up feelings make them unhappy, sometimes even sick.

> Leo's dog, Rex, was killed by a car. Whenever Leo thought about Rex, he just couldn't help crying—even though he had been told "big boys don't cry." Some people didn't think crying was masculine.
>
> Then Leo felt even worse because he was afraid people might call him a "sissy." He was ashamed to feel so sad after Rex's death. He told himself, "Rex was a dumb old dog and I don't even miss him." When Leo locked his sad feelings inside himself, his stomach hurt. Lying to himself just made him feel worse.

It's important to be mindful of our emotions and to work to keep healthy emotionally. You will probably feel better if you go off by yourself and cry when you feel like it. Or you can say to yourself, "Yes, I really feel sad, but if I get busy doing something fun and interesting, maybe my sad feelings will go away." Remember that you can always tell Jesus how you feel in prayer. Jesus knows how we feel because He grew up as a human being just like us (except, of course, without sin). ***Not everyone understands that boys and girls have some of the same feelings.***

It's also important to listen to your own feelings and not worry so much about what other people say. Remember that God loves you just as you are and that God has blessed you with special talents for a reason.

> Ella loved to run and often entered children's races. When Ella was in a race, she put everything she had into winning.
>
> Then someone called Ella a "tomboy." That person didn't think running or sports was feminine. She didn't want to be different from other girls she knew, so she stopped racing. As she watched the boys run, Ella told herself she didn't miss racing at all. But it wasn't true. And she felt so unhappy about giving up racing that she had trouble making friends.

God blesses us with many talents and abilities that are related not to our sex (being male or female) but simply because we're human. Some boys love to draw or play the piano; other boys would rather play baseball or build birdhouses. Some girls like to play soccer or fix bicycles; other girls would rather be cheerleaders or take dancing lessons.

Thank God you have these choices. God has given you many, many talents to which you can bring your uniqueness as a male. If you try a lot of different activities, you will discover many things you are good at, things that make you special. And if you have many different interests, you will have many more ways of making friends.

Remember, *God loves you no matter what*. In fact, God loves you more than you love yourself, and He loves you more than your parents love you! So just be yourself, the terrific, talented person God made. And be yourself, a person with emotions. If you are sad or angry, you can talk about how you feel rather than yell, scream, make demands, or hide yourself away from other people. If you are joyful, hopeful, and excited, you can also express these marvelous feelings with kind words and thoughtful notes or nice actions.

> And Jesus increased in wisdom and in stature and in favor with God and man. (Luke 2:52)
>
> For we do not have a high priest who is unable to sympathize with our weaknesses, but one who in every respect has been tempted as we are, yet without sin. (Hebrews 4:15)
>
> [Jesus] went throughout all Galilee, teaching in their synagogues and proclaiming the gospel of the kingdom and healing every disease and every affliction among the people. (Matthew 4:23)

Dear Jesus, I'm glad You were once a human. You understand what it's like to grow up as a boy. You understand what it's like when people make fun of You and don't understand who You are.

Jesus, sometimes I feel so much pressure to be a male. There's so much expected of me. Remind me that You made me just the way I'm supposed to be, just how You wanted me to be. Remind me that You love me so much that You died for me on the cross and saved me because You didn't want me to be punished as I deserve and because You wanted to be with me forever. Be with me now, Jesus, as I grow up. Amen.

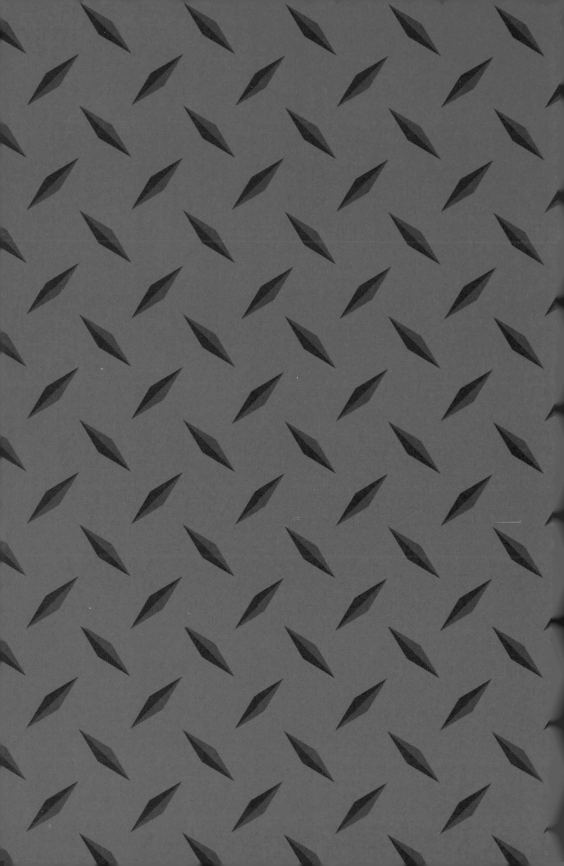

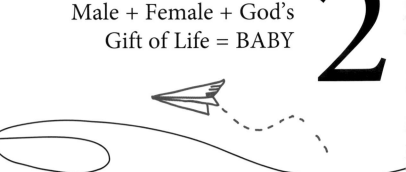

Male + Female + God's Gift of Life = BABY

Men and Women: Alike, Yet Different

If you could see inside the bodies of a man and a woman, you would find much that is alike. In both men and women, the heart pumps blood and the lungs breathe. Many other **organs** work together to keep the person alive. Body parts like the heart, brain, and lungs are called organs. **Sexual organs** do the work of creating new life. They are different in men and women.

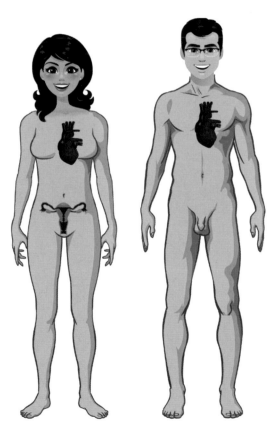

When you began life, you were just one tiny cell, smaller than the dot of an i. This tiny cell that was you was formed when a sperm cell from your father joined an egg cell from your mother.

Under a strong microscope, they'd look about like this:

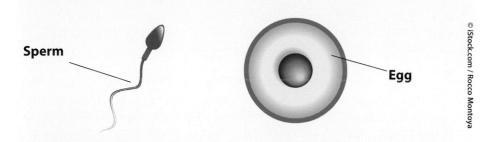

Sperm

Egg

How great God must be, to make a whole person grow from such a tiny beginning! Everyone you know began life in the very same way. That is part of why God made men and women different from each other. Both are needed to bring new life into the world. Both are needed to love, protect, and guide the child they have begun.

A Man's Sexual Organs

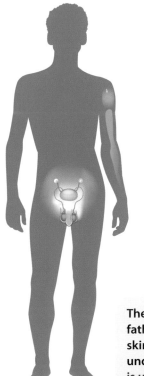

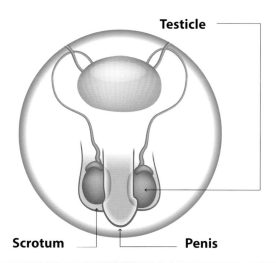

Testicle

Scrotum   Penis

The sperm cell from which you grew was made in one of your father's testicles. There are two roundish testicles in a bag of skin called the **scrotum**. The scrotum hangs just behind and under a man's penis. The penis is a finger-shaped organ, which is usually soft and spongy.

The reproductive organs of boys and men are outside the body: the scrotum (including the testicles) and the penis. In the **testicles** of a grown man, billions of sperm cells grow each month. They are stored in a tube that is in the back of the testicles.

When a boy becomes old enough (approximately between ages 12 and 15), his testicles begin to make sperm cells. His body also makes a milky liquid in which the sperm cells swim. The sperm cells and the milky liquid in which they swim are together called **semen**. Semen leaves the body through the **penis**.

Urine (waste water) also passes from the body through the penis but never at the same time as semen. The **anus**, where bowel movements leave the body, is behind the testicles.

When a girl is between the ages of 10 and 14 (sometimes a little earlier, sometimes a little later), the egg cells in her **ovaries** begin to change and ripen. After that, about once a month, an egg cell leaves one or the other ovary.

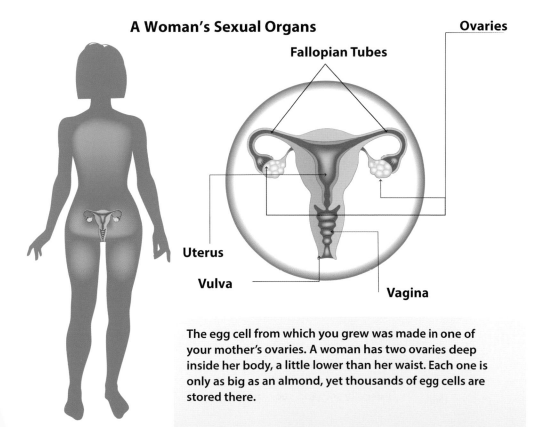

A Woman's Sexual Organs

Ovaries

Fallopian Tubes

Uterus

Vulva

Vagina

The egg cell from which you grew was made in one of your mother's ovaries. A woman has two ovaries deep inside her body, a little lower than her waist. Each one is only as big as an almond, yet thousands of egg cells are stored there.

Near each ovary, a hollow tube, called a **fallopian tube**, opens to receive the egg. While passing through this tube, the egg may meet and unite with a sperm. If it unites with a sperm, the egg continues its journey to the **uterus**, or **womb**. If it does not join a sperm, the egg disintegrates.

The uterus lies between the ovaries and just above the bone that forms a bridge between a girl's legs. It is about the size and shape of a pear. This organ can stretch like a balloon to many times its ordinary size. It is here that a fertilized egg cell grows into a baby.

The uterus is connected to the outside of the body by a narrow passageway. This organ, the **vagina**, opens between the legs. It is covered by folds of skin and flesh called the **vulva**. The opening through which urine passes is also within the vulva, and in the back is the anus, where solid waste leaves the body.

The ovaries, fallopian tubes, uterus, vagina, and vulva are the **reproductive organs** of girls and women. All except the vulva are inside the body.

A Brand-New Person

When a sperm cell from your father met and united with an egg cell in one of your mother's fallopian tubes, your life began. In that instant, the question of whether you were going to be a boy or a girl was decided. There are many sperm cells in a man's semen. About half of them are able to start a boy baby; about half are able to start a girl baby. It all depends on which sperm cell joins the egg cell.

The egg cell and the sperm cell did more than just stick together. Following God's design, the two cells changed into one new cell—the be-

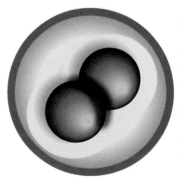

ginning of a brand-new person! That tiny life had all the genetic information that makes a person unique—that makes you ***you***. That cell had its own, one-of-a-kind code (DNA) that acted like an instruction manual for how you would develop. So whatever you look like, whatever your abilities, whatever your personality, it is all designed by God!

At the moment the cells joined, the speck of new life was male; it had in it the color of your hair, the shape of your nose, and the talents that would someday help make you special. That's why you look a little bit like your mother and a little bit like your father.

A woman's body makes thousands of egg cells in her lifetime. Each of those egg cells has different **genes**, different directions for making a baby. A man makes billions of sperm cells in his lifetime; each one has different genes in it. Your **characteristics**, things like straight hair and blue eyes, were decided by the particular genes in the sperm cell that happened to join the genes in a particular egg cell.

Your genes determine who you are going to be, but *your experiences are also important in making you the person you are*. For example, if you have fun going fishing with your grandfather and try hard to follow his directions when you fish together, you might be more likely to be a good fisherman. Your experiences, your learning, and your hard work will always be an important part of you. You can't change the color of your eyes, but you can become a better reader. You can learn to control your quick temper.

Everyone is born with both strengths and weaknesses. With God's help, you can discover your strengths—your best characteristics—and work to develop them. And, with God's help, you can learn ways to overcome or compensate for your weaknesses.

A Masterpiece

Praise God that He created us—male and female—in His image (Genesis 1:27, 31), an image that is being restored in us through the grace and mercy of Christ Jesus. This doesn't mean that we have a physical resemblance to God, like you share the same color of eyes as your dad. It means that *we reflect God's character*. Has anyone ever told you "the apple doesn't fall far from the tree"? They were probably saying that you have similar mannerisms or act in some of the same ways as your dad or mom. The same is true of you and your heavenly Father. How would you describe God? Loving? Caring? Holy? Before the fall into sin, humans were pure and free from evil too. After the fall into sin, we rely on Jesus to make everything perfect again.

You are delightful—just the way God wanted you to be—but because of sin, things are no longer perfect. Thankfully, through Christ, God already sees you as perfect. And one day, we will have perfect, new bodies for our life in heaven. We, "beholding the glory of the Lord, are being transformed into the same image" (2 Corinthians 3:18).

Until that day, you are being "transformed by the renewal of your mind, that by testing you may discern what is the will of God, what is good and acceptable and perfect" (Romans 12:2). Right now, we bear the image of sinful Adam, but we will bear the image of the perfect "man of heaven," Jesus (1 Corinthians 15:49). God is at work in us now, and on the day of Christ, He will bring it to completion (Philippians 1:6).

Each artist has his or her own style and favorite colors, subjects, and the like. You can tell things about the artist based on the artwork; his or her personality is reflected in the artwork. God is the artist who lovingly designed you. You can see His handiwork and personality reflected in you! You are valued because you were created in God's image. You are worthy of dignity and respect! What the Maker of heaven and earth has created is very good. The Bible calls you a masterpiece, God's "workmanship" (Ephesians 2:10).

You Are an Important Part of a Family

Your family is another one of God's gifts to you—and you are God's gift to your family. Whether you are an only child, the oldest child, a middle one, or the youngest, your family would not be complete without you. God created you and placed you in a family to love and take care of you. Sometimes, because of sin, our families don't always love and care for us the way God would like. But it is most important to remember that God is your heavenly Father, and He gave you Jesus to die for you and to bring you to live with Him someday. He hears you when you pray to Him. He helps you in ways you expect and don't expect. You can always trust in God; He is your Creator!

Sometimes, a child thinks someone else is the parents' favorite. Parents do not treat all their children in the same way because each child is a unique individual with different abilities, concerns, and problems. Parents treat each child a little differently because each child is special. Your parents probably try hard to meet your individual needs.

Families begin when God brings a man and woman together and they decide to get married. They plan to live their lives together. They promise

© iStock.com / Adrian Hillman

to be together and take care of each other for as long as they live. This is God's plan, as Jesus states in Mark 10:6–9, that "from the beginning of creation, 'God made them male and female.' Therefore a man shall leave his father and mother and hold fast to his wife, and the two shall become one flesh. So they are no longer two but one flesh. What therefore God has joined together, let not man separate."

God made a husband and a wife to complement each other and to bring out the best in each other as they form a family. They are like puzzle pieces that perfectly match each other to form a beautiful scene.

God instituted (established) marriage because He knew what a blessing it is to bring happiness and fulfillment to our lives. A husband and a wife are like a team, working together to create a loving, healthy home and encouraging and strengthening each other. How much more two can accomplish (Ecclesiastes 4:9)! What a support when one is feeling weak! God shows His love for us through the love of our spouse.

A husband and wife are best friends who share companionship and similar interests and values. God blessed marriage for the procreation of children, who are to be brought up in the Lord and to offer Him their praise (Genesis 1:28). A home is a wonderful, safe place to share happy times, laughter, learning experiences, and to provide support for each other during difficult times.

A husband and wife are best friends who support each other. A husband and wife find happiness in giving themselves for the other person; they respect each other and find joy in putting their spouse's needs before their own needs.

A husband and wife find peace and contentment and feel emotionally healthy because they trust that their spouse loves them and wants to be committed only to him or her for their entire life together. And they always have someone to share their thoughts with . . . someone who will be there when they need it and who will always love them, no matter what. A husband and wife find delight in each other.

But we are all sinners—grown-ups too. Husbands and wives won't always agree, so you may hear your parents talk through some of those differences. Husbands and wives will sometimes disappoint each other. Marriage is where we learn to forgive and find forgiveness from the one who has committed to love us even in hard times. There are many in the world who want to get rid of people, or judge and condemn those who make mistakes, but a godly marriage is a place where you can make mistakes and also grow and learn with the support of a loving wife.

Marriage is so special that God gives the best picture of what it should be like. He says that Jesus is the Bridegroom and the Church (all believers) is the Bride. Jesus calls the Church beautiful, and He was willing to die for the Church. "Greater love has no one than this, that someone lay down his life for his friends" (John 15:13). In marriage vows, a husband promises to cherish and care for his wife. A wife promises to love and honor her husband.

Not all families have a mother and a father. Sometimes sad things happen, such as the death of a husband or wife or divorce, when the husband and wife separate from each other and end the marriage. Children in these families often feel that whatever happened must be partly their fault. But there is nothing a child can do to cause a divorce, and there is nothing a child can do to stop such things from happening. There is no way a child can make divorced people want to get married again. It is very sad, but families get broken. Talk to Jesus about any sadness you may ever feel. We know from the Bible that Mary, His mom, was with Him when He died, but His father, Joseph, was not. It may be that His earthly father had already died.

It's important to remember that all families have hard times. God is there in good times and in bad. He is always ready to forgive us and to bless us in ways we might not even expect.

No family is perfect. People are never exactly as we would like them to be. But God will help you accept the people in your family as they are. He will help you love and support each other. He will help your love grow. 1 John 4:11 reminds us, "If God so loved us, we also ought to love one another."

God's Plan for New Life

A woman and a man get married because they love each other very much. Each of them has found a special friend, much better than any friend they have ever had. And they show their love in many ways. They help each other. They share happy times and sad times. They enjoy just being together. Each married couple has their own favorite ways of showing love for each other.

At times, a husband and wife will want to express their love for each other in a special, physical way called sexual **intercourse**, which many people shorten and call "having sex" (or you may hear "making love"). At those times, they will go off by themselves. They will hug and kiss each other and touch each other all over. The husband's penis will become firm and hard, able to fit inside his wife's vagina. This is to be a private act between husband and wife.

While they are loving each other in this way, semen comes out of the husband's penis. Many sperm cells are in the semen. The sperm cells move up the vagina, through the uterus, and into the fallopian tubes leading to the ovaries. If one sperm cell joins an egg cell in a fallopian tube, new life is started. A baby begins to develop.

A baby does not begin to grow every time a husband and wife have sex. An egg cell is in one of the fallopian tubes only a few days each month, and only then can a baby be started.

This may sound very strange or even gross to you now, but for adults who love each other, it's actually something nice and pleasant. As your body changes and develops, your ideas and feelings about your body will change too.

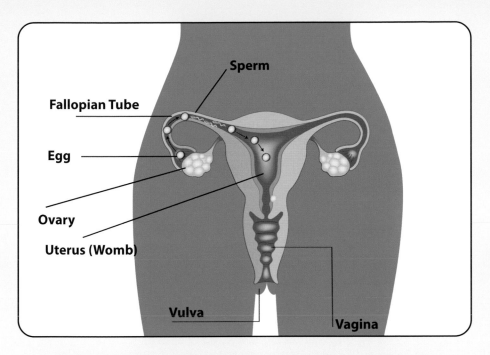

Labels on diagram: Sperm, Fallopian Tube, Egg, Ovary, Uterus (Womb), Vulva, Vagina

God wants only a husband and his wife to make love in this way.
People who are not married who have sex are breaking God's commandments (Exodus 20:14). They have turned away from God's will and put their own will above God's. This is sinful and leads to many troubles. When books, movies, TV shows, and even some "friends" say this is okay, we should remember that God comes first in our lives and so we obey Him. He knows what is best for us. He is the one who created us and designed us this way! And He is the one who loves us the most.

People who are not married who have sex might not be thinking of all the heartache and consequences that happen since they are going away from God's perfect plan. They may only be thinking of themselves and may not be thinking about the future.

If an unmarried man and woman try to use sex to become closer to each other or to feel good about themselves, they will be disappointed and hurt. When you are married, sex shows that you are connected and united in body and spirit to only one person. But when you are not married and have sex, you may have doubts about your relationship with that person and you may feel insecure about what the person (and others) feel about you. Instead of making you feel better or making your relationship stronger, it only makes you feel worse and weakens your relationship.

There is no commitment, and that way of thinking about sex can harm your future marriage.

If an unmarried man and woman have children together because they have been having sex before marriage, there are many challenges financially and emotionally. Husbands and wives have promised to live together always and to make a home for their children. As parents, they will take care of the babies born to them.

Some people decide not to have any children. Some others cannot have children because their sexual organs do not work as they should. Some couples without children want children enough to adopt a child whose birth parents could not take care of him or her.

> The word of the LORD came to me, saying, "Before I formed you in the womb I knew you, and before you were born I consecrated you." (Jeremiah 1:4–5)

Dear God, This all sounds so strange, yet amazing and wonderful to me that You would design life to start in this way. I trust that You know what's best for me, since You designed me! If it's Your will, please bless me with a special woman to marry—someone who will love me and love You.

Thank You for the friends I have now, God. Teach me to be the kind of friend that I'd like to have. Help me get ready for the day when I begin a close, fulfilling, lifelong friendship with my wife. Amen.

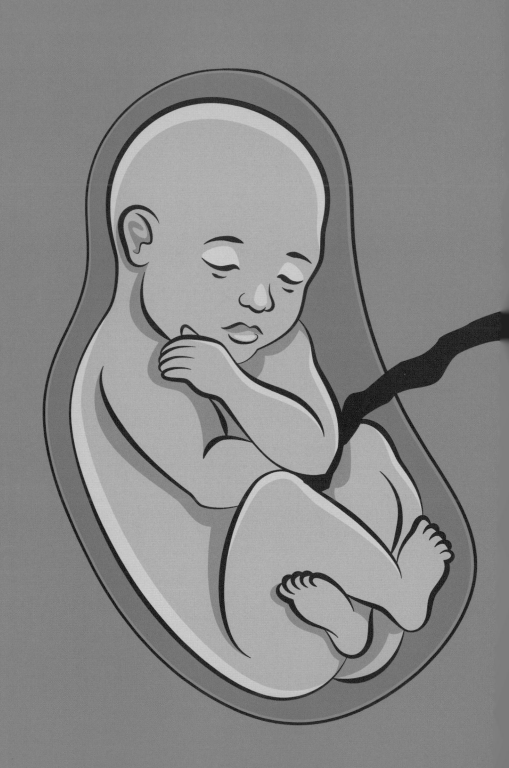

God Took Care of You . . . Right from the Beginning 3

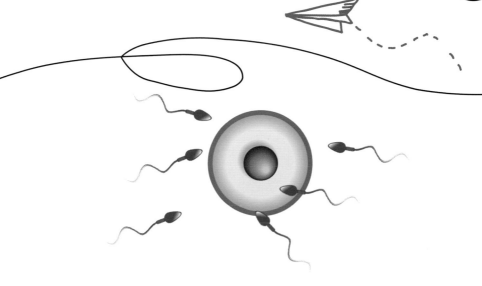

Smaller Than a Dot

When the sperm cell from your father joined the egg cell in your mother, you were really smaller than the dot on this i!

Soon, something wonderful happened. That one cell that was you divided into two cells. All at once, you were twice as big as you had been.

During the next few weeks, you doubled your size again and again. You also moved from the fallopian tube to the uterus, where God had prepared a safe and comfortable place for you to live and grow. (See the drawing on page 33.)

When you had been growing for only three to four weeks, you had a tiny beating heart. And at about two months, you were a little more than an inch long and you already started moving. Your head was very big compared to your body because so much was already developing there. You had short arms and legs and fingers and toes. You had the beginnings of a stomach and a brain. At three months, it was already possible to tell you were going to be a boy. At that time, you were also able to grasp with your fingers.

You floated in a bag full of a liquid that was mostly water (called **amniotic fluid**). The water acted like a springy cushion, protecting you from bumps. You were always just warm enough. Very hot days or cold days didn't bother you a bit.

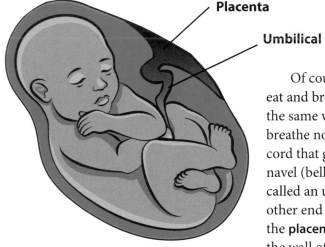

Placenta

Umbilical Cord

Of course, you couldn't eat and breathe in the water the same way you eat and breathe now. Do you see the cord that goes to the baby's navel (belly button)? It is called an umbilical cord. The other end of the cord joins the **placenta**, an organ on the wall of the uterus.

Your blood flowed into the placenta. Food and oxygen moved from your mother's blood to yours. Waste materials from your body went into your mother's amniotic fluid.

When you had been growing for about four and a half months, you began acting more and more like a newborn baby. You began to suck your thumb, so you would know how to suck for milk after you were born. Still inside the bag of water, you were big enough to push against the walls of the uterus as you kicked and stretched your arms and legs. For the first time, your mother could feel the little flutter inside her when you moved. What a thrilling moment that was for her!

Most **pregnant** women have a checkup about once a month to see how the baby is getting along. (The word *pregnant* means that a woman has a baby growing in her uterus.) In time, you were big enough for the doctor to hear your heartbeat with a stethoscope. With a special ultrasound machine, doctors can see how the baby is developing (growing) in the uterus. The image seen on the machine is called a **sonogram**. The doctor or technician can take a picture to show the baby to the mother and father and brothers and sisters. The sonogram can also show whether the baby is a boy or a girl.

The Last Few Months before Birth

As you grew still bigger, your mother's belly, also known as the abdomen, became big and round. Her uterus stretched to give you more room, but you had to lie more and more tightly curled up. Your mother knew when you were asleep, because when you were awake, you kicked harder against the wall of the uterus.

Although your eyes were still tightly shut, your ears were beginning to work. Loud noises made you jump, and you listened all day to your mother's heartbeat. Sometimes, you even had hiccups. In some ways, the people in your family felt the way you do when you are waiting for Christmas. They could hardly wait for you to be born. They asked all sorts of questions: Will our baby be a boy or a girl? Whom will he or she look like? What name shall we choose?

Everyone helped get ready for the big day. Your parents probably fixed a special place for you to sleep. They got baby clothes and diapers and little blankets ready. Your father and sisters and brothers tried to be extra helpful so your mother could get extra rest. She got tired carrying you around all day!

Your mother packed a little suitcase of clothes for both of you. She wanted to be ready when the time came to go to the hospital where you would be born.

Finally, the Great Day Came

After about nine months, you were ready to be born. The uterus began to squeeze and push you out, very gently at first and then with more and more power. Slowly, you moved down into the vagina and out through the vulva.

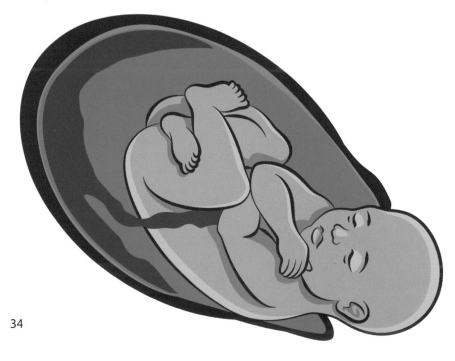

34

The bag of water broke, and the vagina and vulva stretched to let you come out between your mother's legs. This was very slow, hard work for your mother. The muscles that squeezed and stretched got very tired, so tired they hurt. But your mother was happy and excited because she was about to see you for the first time. The long months of waiting were almost over. Soon, she would hold you in her arms.

In some situations, mothers have a **Cesarean delivery** (also known as a C-section), where the mother has surgery. The baby is delivered when a doctor makes a small cut in the mother's abdomen and uterus. This is more common if the mother is thirty-five-years-old or older.

Most babies are born in hospitals, but it is possible for a mother to give birth to a healthy baby at home or a birthing center. Doctors and nurses help make the mother and baby more comfortable. The baby's father often helps too. More and more women are getting help and support from a trained caregiver such as a midwife or doula, who help women and their families before, during, and after labor.

The mother and the father want to hold the baby as soon as possible, but first the doctor must make sure that the baby is breathing. Usually, the baby begins to cry, and no wonder! The baby is still wet from the amniotic fluid, and the room is much colder than the mother's body was.

Once the baby begins breathing, it no longer needs the placenta or the umbilical cord. So the doctor cuts the cord. Cutting the cord doesn't hurt the mother or the baby; it's like cutting hair or fingernails.

Soon after the baby is born, the mother's uterus pushes out the placenta. The mother's uterus, vagina, and vulva slowly return to their normal size.

Soon, the mother's breasts will begin to make milk. In most cases, there will be enough milk to feed the baby for a long time. When the baby no longer sucks at her breasts because he drinks from a bottle or a cup, the mother's breasts will stop making milk.

Most babies are not very pretty right after they are born. Often, the head has been pushed into an odd shape during birth. The skin is wrinkled and red. After a few days, the skin becomes a normal color, and the soft bones of the head move back into shape. But the family usually thinks their baby is beautiful, right from the first day! In God's eyes, all babies are beautiful and wonderful. Jesus had a special love for children. Jesus said, "Let the little children come to Me and do not hinder them, for to such belongs the kingdom of heaven" (Matthew 19:14).

Human babies are helpless long after birth. ***Babies need not only food, warmth, and safety, but also love from both a father and a mother.*** A baby who is never held or talked to would get sick and might even die. When babies are older, they still need someone who will love them and help them learn and grow. That's why God's plan for families is so important. Babies and children need parents who will love and care for them for many years.

Premature Babies

God designed it that after nine months in the uterus, babies are ready to live in the world. Babies born before they have been in the uterus nine months are called **premature** babies. They can grow to be strong and healthy—but they need extra care after they are born. They are usually kept for a while in **incubators**, which keep them warm and away from germs. Although it's not the way God designed it to be the most healthy, babies have been known to live if they were born at twenty-two or twenty-three weeks. Babies who have not been born yet (at first called an **embryo** and then at three months called a **fetus**) are living people; it's just best if they develop inside their mother for forty weeks.

Twins

Once in a while, a mother will have two or more babies on the same day. Isn't it amazing that her uterus will stretch enough to make room for them as they grow?! Sometimes, the uterus gets too crowded; then, these babies are born a little early. Of course, two babies can't come out at the same time, so one is always a few minutes older than the other.

There are two kinds of twins, **fraternal twins** and **identical twins**. Fraternal twins begin life when two different sperm cells join two different egg cells. Fraternal twins are not much more alike than any other two children in the same family. They might be two boys, two girls, or a boy and a girl.

Identical twins begin life when one sperm cell joins one egg cell. The one new cell splits into two cells, then each begins to develop separately as two different people. Identical twins look exactly alike, but they are not. Each one is special. Each has his or her own interests, ideas, personalities, and experiences.

Taking Care of Our Bodies

What a great responsibility it is to be pregnant! God entrusts a whole new life to the mother. ***Whatever the mother does affects the unborn baby.*** That's why it's so important for the mother to take care of her own body, especially when she's pregnant. Mothers-to-be should not smoke, drink alcohol, or take drugs because these can cause serious harm to an unborn baby. Whatever the mother takes into her body is shared (unfortunately, in some cases) with her baby.

For instance, doctors have learned that an unborn baby's heart beats much faster after the mother smokes a cigarette. When pregnant women smoke, they can do serious damage to the health of their babies. Similarly, babies and children suffer harmful effects when living in a household where one or both parents smoke.

You already know that you feel better and look better if you eat right, get enough sleep and exercise, and stay away from drugs that might be harmful. Now, you have another reason to take care of your body. If you decide to have a child someday, you will already have formed the good habits that will help everyone in your family enjoy good health.

> **My frame was not hidden from You, when I was being made in secret, intricately woven in the depths of the earth. Your eyes saw my unformed substance. (Psalm 139:15–16)**

Lord, You have taken care of me all my life. You have always been with me . . . loving me, ready to listen. You know me better than I know myself. How wonderful You are!

I know You remember the day I was born, God. I wish I could remember. I wonder what I first noticed in this strange new world. I wonder what my family said when they saw me for the first time.

Yes, You remember the day I was born—and the days before that. If You knew me when I was a tiny speck inside my mother, You surely know me now.

You know my likes and dislikes. You know whether I feel terrific or terrible . . . and You care. You can even look into the future and see the grown-up person I will be someday.

I don't understand how You can know me so well, God, and still love me, but I'm glad You do. And I know You love me because You sent Your Son, Jesus, to be born in our sinful world. It's strange and wonderful to think that Jesus, too, was once only the size of a speck! Thank You for sending Jesus to be a human so that He could die on the cross to take away my sins. Because of Jesus, I know we will be together now and forever in heaven. Amen.

You've Grown!

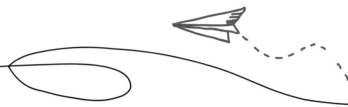

It's amazing to think of how you grew as a baby, but it's also special to think of all the ways you're growing now. ***The most important growing happens inside a person.*** You'll grow on the outside too, when your body is ready. But right now, you are growing on the inside.

When the Holy Spirit called you through God's Word and Baptism, God made you a member of His family. Now, as you learn more about Jesus, you are growing as a Christian . . . growing in your faith.

And Jesus helps you. He is with you and has given you the gift of the Holy Spirit. "The fruit of the Spirit is love, joy, peace, patience, kindness, goodness, faithfulness, gentleness, self-control" (Galatians 5:22–23). Because of your growing faith and your growing maturity, you do things like setting the dinner table or taking care of younger siblings when your parents are busy. You notice when your parents are tired, and you try to help them. You make a special birthday card for someone you love or just surprise him or her with an extra hug.

A part of growing up is feeling like you'd rather be with your friends or be alone than be with your family. When you were a baby, you wanted to be with your mother all the time. Even when you began to go to school, it was hard to be away from home so much of the day.

But now, you like to stay all night at a friend's house. Maybe you've gone somewhere—like to a camp—by yourself, even though none of your friends were going. Or maybe your family moved, and you went to a new school where you didn't know anyone. Being by yourself may have been hard at first, especially if it seemed like everyone else but you had a friend to be with, but hopefully over time, you were able to make new friends and grow in your confidence.

Although you may be searching for your own identity apart from your parents, it's important to keep communicating with them and to learn from them. Another part of growing up is talking about the changes that are happening or going to happen in your body. It may be embarrassing to talk to your parents about those changes or about sex—and they may be embarrassed too—but it gets easier the more you talk to them. It's wise to talk about important things—like sex and how God designed our bodies—with people who care enough about you to make sure you understand everything correctly. Your friends won't know all the right answers, and you can't trust everything you read on the Internet. And not having the right information about sex now could affect your entire future.

Some people have mixed-up and sinful ideas about sex and the body. Oftentimes, TV shows and songs on the radio do not show God's design for sex to be something special, reserved only for marriage. People talk about living for the moment and wanting to feel good at that time, but they don't think about long-term consequences. Part of growing up is understanding the feeling inside of you that what you're doing or listening to or talking about isn't what pleases God, and then having the courage to stop doing it or listening to it or talking about it.

God intentionally made our bodies beautiful and good and interesting. *You can feel good about your body because you know God created it.* You can thank God for its creation in words God's people have used for thousands of years: "I praise You, for I am fearfully and wonderfully made. Wonderful are Your works; my soul knows it very well" (Psalm 139:14). Having a healthy understanding of yourself and your body and sexuality is an important reminder that you are God's child and you look to God for identity and meaning rather than turning to the world to tell you how special you are. The world has so many confusing messages about these things.

The Holy Spirit will help you give your body the best of care and will guide you to respect your body as God would like you to. The Holy Spirit will lead you to respect other people and their bodies too. Part of growing up is taking more interest in how you look. It's great to take time to look your best, and as your body grows in the next few years, the physical changes might mean changes in your hygiene and in the way you get ready each day.

One change in your body is that the sweat glands start to send out chemicals that can make sweat smell stronger. Body odor is a result of sweat and bacteria on your skin. It's important to shower daily and to wash your sports uniforms after each game or practice. Take your shoes and sweaty pads or other equipment out of your gym bag so they can air dry when you get home. Spraying air freshener on your gear will also help. Now is the time to start wearing deodorant or antiperspirant. Antiperspirants stop the sweat and deodorants stop the smell; some products do both.

Sweating is also usually the cause of jock itch, when a fungus develops in the groin or inner thighs. You might notice a raised rash with what looks like dry, flaky skin around the edges of the rash, and you might feel itching or burning. The fungus that causes jock itch can be spread, and it's common for it to start as athlete's foot and move to the groin area. Be sure to clean the infected areas well and dry thoroughly; then, put on an antifungal cream or spray.

Other new things you might notice happening with your body include the onset of **acne**. Acne can be caused by overgrowth of skin, clogged pores, oil production, and bacteria. Some doctors call it a developmental condition because *most young people get acne*. Your body makes hormones that make your face oily, and oil glands in the face are usually more active in boys than girls.

Instead of scrubbing the skin, use your hands to gently wash your face with a mild soap and water. You can use a product with salicylic acid or benzoyl peroxide. Have patience when treating acne; you have many layers of skin, and it may take months to see results.

Boys, in particular, are more prone to getting acne on their back. Your back has glands on it that can lead to clogged pores, especially—you guessed it—if sweating is involved. Again, be sure to clean your skin daily and use a soap that contains benzoyl peroxide, if necessary.

Besides body odor caused by sweating, *you may start to feel more conscious about your mouth having an odor* (bad breath). This is often caused by not taking good care of your teeth and gums. Prevent bad breath by brushing (including your tongue) and flossing regularly, using breath mints, and of course, avoiding cigarettes.

Although it's important to take care of your God-given body, it's also important not to dwell on your looks and not to think about your appearance all the time. Jesus gives many reminders in the Bible that we are not to worry about what we will wear. And "man looks on the outward appearance, but the LORD looks on the heart" (1 Samuel 16:7). It is your loving spirit and the ways you serve others that make you truly attractive (1 Peter 3:4).

You want people to notice you for who you are—for your personality—not for what you look like. Wear clothes that will not draw attention to the parts that are private. We protect and honor the goodness of the body, especially those special parts that God created to bring forth new life.

When you present yourself in a way that doesn't draw attention to yourself, you are being modest. Being modest can include not only the way you dress, but your thoughts and actions too. As you grow in your faith, the Holy Spirit will guide you and give you the self-control you need to act properly and decently. Remember, Jesus is at work in you, creating a pure (blameless, without sin) heart.

We are reminded in Matthew 15:19 that "out of the heart come evil thoughts, . . . sexual immorality." Sexual immorality includes the things you think or do that are outside of God's design for sex. This includes having sex before you are married, thinking sexual thoughts about other people, or looking at images about sex on the Internet that cause you to think or do these things. But we also know that as we are forgiven by Jesus' saving actions and as we are sanctified by the working of the Holy Spirit, God leads us to new life. That allows us to follow the advice of the apostle Paul: "Whatever is true, whatever is honorable, whatever is just, whatever is pure, whatever is lovely, whatever is commendable, if there is any excellence, if there is anything worthy of praise, think about these things" (Philippians 4:8).

> But grow in the grace and knowledge of our Lord and Savior Jesus Christ. To Him be the glory both now and to the day of eternity! Amen. (2 Peter 3:18)

Dear Lord, I'm growing. In some ways I'm growing too fast, and in some ways I'm growing too slow.

Help me not to be so worried. The too-fasts, too-slows, too-smalls, and too-bigs are based less on facts and more on my feelings. I'm thankful that this is all in Your hands. It's exciting to know that You have designed me just right and that You are giving me just the right experiences today that will help me in the future.

Lord, You know what is best for me, and Your timing is always best. After all, You said, "I know the plans I have for you . . . plans for welfare and not for evil, to give you a future and a hope" (Jeremiah 29:11). You're amazing!

Someday I'll be grown up—soon enough. Help me to focus now on who I am today, a child of God. Guide me throughout my whole life to grow emotionally, socially, intelligently, and above all, spiritually.

Each day, lead me to look to You, dear Lord, as the one who created, redeemed, and comforts me in body and soul. Thank You for sending the Holy Spirit to guide me, strengthen me, and work through me to live according to Your will. Amen.

Next Step: Adolescence 5

A Time of Change

The years when a person changes from a child to an adult are called **adolescence**. Although we think of adolescents as teenagers, some people begin this time of change as early as nine or ten years old. **Puberty *is the name of this first stage in adolescence, when a person first becomes physically capable of having a baby.***

This chapter will talk about those changes in your body, but remember that while your body is physically able to produce new life, you are still growing in the other areas of your life. God is helping you to develop into a responsible adult so that one day you might become a parent yourself. But remember that adolescence continues throughout your teenage years. And most scientists who study the brain agree that the prefrontal cortex (the part that helps you make wise decisions) in your brain is not fully developed until you are about twenty-five years old.

At this point in your life, many children try to rush into having adult privileges and responsibilities, but many other children find it hard to believe that they will ever be interested in the other sex. The idea of changing into a grown-up person seems very strange to them.

But whether these children like the idea or not, adults who say they will change are right. In a few years, boys will probably begin to like girls in a new and special way. When a boy is near a certain girl, he may feel uncomfortable and happy and shy and excited—all at the same time. A girl is likely to have the same feelings when she's with a special boy. Strong feelings are a part of these growing-up years. One day, you might feel on top of the world; the next day, you might feel very unhappy.

If you have an adolescent brother or sister, you know that people of this age are often hard to live with. They may burst into tears or slam doors for no reason that anyone else can see. They are so busy growing up, they may forget to be patient with younger children in the family. Sometimes they are unpredictable—you don't know what to expect next.

When you get to this stage yourself or if your friends reach this point first, remember that your identity is that you are a child of God. **Your value is not found in who likes you, but in who God made you to be.** Spend your time on your other interests. Instead of dwelling on girls, focus your time on developing your talents and skills in sports and music and academics. You'll be happier focusing on how you can do things to help other people rather than focusing on the opposite sex.

Adolescents usually want more independence than their parents are ready to give them. You may start to feel that you want more freedom to go places on your own or watch more mature movies and TV shows. It's hard for adolescents to wait until parents are convinced they are responsible enough to handle more freedom, but it's important to listen to your parents and to share how you are feeling. Your parents are a gift from God so that they can continue to take care of you and teach you things about life. You may feel like you're ready to try new things, but keep in mind that your brain is not yet ready to emotionally handle adult content.

During adolescence, you may find that sometimes you want to be older, to be powerful and adventurous and independent—but sometimes you're a little unsure about the new responsibilities and experiences. As you start to see your body beginning to change, sometimes you might like to keep on being a child. That's normal, and besides talking to your parents, you can always talk to your Father in heaven about all of these feelings. He will always listen and always care.

How Boys Change

Boys usually have their time of fast growth a couple years later than girls do. A boy may grow very fast for a year or two, then continue to grow more slowly until he is twenty or so. Your hands and your feet will be the first part of your body to grow, and then your arms, legs, and rest of your body. Sometimes, your body will grow so fast that your tendons and ligaments become tighter. Tendons connect muscle to bone and ligaments connect bone to bone or cartilage to bone. Some people call this tightness and achiness **growing pains**. One way to decrease the pain is to be sure to stretch before and after exercise.

As your body goes through such rapid growth, you may find yourself more hungry. Before puberty, boys eat about 1,800 to 2,200 calories per day. Boys in their teens need about 600 calories more, about 2,400 to 2,800! Boys who are active in sports need even more calories. This is normal and healthy; your body needs more energy and nutrients to support your development.

As you begin growing taller and heavier, other changes will take place in your body. Usually the first sign of puberty is that your testicles will get bigger because they are beginning to make sperm cells. Most adolescent boys are more comfortable if they wear an **athletic supporter** when they participate in active sports. Athletic supporters are a kind of underpants that are elastic and hold the testicles and penis close to the body, where these sensitive organs are less likely to be hurt. Depending on the sport, you might instead wear an athletic cup (that fits over and protects the penis and testicles) and compression shorts.

The next change is that your voice begins to change. When you reach puberty, your body begins to make a male hormone called **testosterone**. This hormone causes your voice box to grow and your vocal cords to get thicker and longer, which makes your voice sound deeper. As your body is changing, your voice may crack. You can hear this change in your body, but you can also see it. When the voice box grows, part of it sticks out from your neck; this is called your **Adam's apple**. This process will not last forever; it will most likely take several months.

Next, hair will begin to grow around your penis and under your arms. This is called **pubic hair**. Then your penis will become bigger, your shoulders broader, and your muscles more powerful. And then finally, as time goes on, you will notice hair beginning to grow above your upper lip. More hair will appear on your chin; soon, you will be ready to shave for the first time. Shave after a warm shower, and use shaving cream or gel. Shave in the same direction your hair grows and use short, light strokes.

Another change that happens sometime during puberty is that you will have **erections** more often than you did when you were little. When you have an erection, your penis becomes erect—that is, instead of being limp and soft, it becomes hard and stands out from your body. Often, there is no reason for the erection. It just happens. In a few minutes, the penis goes back to its usual size. As you grow older, you will have more control over your penis. These erections will happen at different times of the day and even while you sleep.

When you are somewhere between ages 12 and 15, you are old enough to have **ejaculations**—semen being released from your penis. Often, this happens when you are asleep. Sometimes, it's called a **wet dream**, or **nocturnal emission**, because you may have an exciting dream about a girl at the same time. When you wake up, you may find a wet, sticky spot on your underwear or pajamas.

There is no reason to feel guilty or embarrassed about any part of a wet dream. Wet dreams are normal, and you can't control them. Your body is starting to produce testosterone, and once it makes the hormone, it can release sperm. When you wake up, simply clean yourself with soap and water. Wipe off the semen on your clothes or bedding with some tissue, but don't worry about it. Parents know that adolescent boys have wet dreams.

When you have your first ejaculation, you will know you have taken a step toward becoming a man. Of course, it is only a first step. Although your body is getting ready for fatherhood, your mind and spirit still have a lot of growing to do. And testosterone levels are their highest late in puberty, so boys might be tempted to do more reckless or aggressive things. Remember to be aware of your emotions and what triggers those strong feelings; continue to pray for good judgment and self-control.

Even more important than the physical changes on the steps toward manhood are the matters of growing in responsibility, integrity, maturity in decision making, and wisdom as God's Spirit guides you. Talk with your parents about each of these key steps. With God's blessing, you will continue to grow in faith as His own dear child.

Remember that throughout all these changes, God is with you and He will never change. As the Bible says, "Jesus Christ is the same yesterday and today and forever" (Hebrews 13:8). His forgiveness, love, compassion, and blessing are constant. Nothing will change the fact that because of Jesus, you will be made perfect, as God always intended you to be. You will have a perfect body and perfect life in heaven because of Jesus. On His return, "the trumpet will sound, and the dead will be raised imperishable, and we shall be changed" (1 Corinthians 15:52).

How Girls Change

When a girl begins to grow up, the shape of her body changes. Her breasts and hips slowly become larger. **Breast buds** are a slight elevation and enlargement of the nipple area. Hair grows near her sexual organs and under her arms too. Within one to three years, she might be six to eight inches taller and quite a bit heavier.

About two years after her breasts begin to develop, another important change takes place. An egg cell will move from one of her ovaries to her uterus. Her body sends extra blood to the uterus, so it will be ready to feed the new life that would begin if that egg cell should join a sperm cell. A soft new lining grows all over the inside of the uterus. When girls reach puberty, their body begins to make a female hormone called **estrogen**. This hormone helps you to build strong bones, and it also makes the lining of the uterus grow and thicken.

When no baby is started, the egg cell, the new lining, and the extra blood aren't needed. They break up and flow out though the vagina. This is called **menstruation**, and it happens about once a month to nearly every woman. The unneeded material is mostly blood, and that's what it looks like. Since we think of being hurt when we see blood, menstruation can be scary for a girl who does not understand what is happening. But this is all extra blood that her body does not need, and it comes out very slowly.

Females wear disposable **sanitary napkins** (also called **maxi pads**) or **tampons** to catch the blood. They may also wear a small, thin pad called a **pantiliner** when it's been a little less than a month since their last period. Some girls have mild pains below their waist (called **cramps** because the muscles of the uterus are contracting). Because a girl's body is producing hormones, she may feel moody, especially the days right before her period. This is called premenstrual syndrome, or **PMS**. She may feel more anxious or irritable, and she may even feel like eating differently.

A woman's **period** (the time when she is menstruating) lasts about three to seven days. It often takes several years before a young girl has a period every month. At first, there might be several months between her periods. The first menstrual period of a girl is called menarche. These changes are the creation and blessing of God, and we should respect the unique growth and development of every individual.

Although the time of the first menstruation may be as early as age 9 or 10, it may not be until as late as age 17 or 18. After that, she will usually menstruate every four weeks until she is forty-five or fifty years old, unless she is pregnant. When a baby is growing in her uterus, the extra blood and the soft new lining are needed for the baby.

> **Every good gift and every perfect gift is from above, coming down from the Father of lights with whom there is no variation or shadow due to change. (James 1:17)**

Dear God, all these changes that are going to be happening to my body can seem overwhelming at times. How will I ever get used to my new, more grown-up body? Sometimes I feel like the changes are happening too slowly, and sometimes I feel like they're happening too fast. Thank You for promising to be with me and to take my cares and burdens upon Yourself.

I trust that Your plan for the way people become adults is best. It's wonderful to think that You designed it this way so that one day I could become a husband and a father. Thanks for giving me time to prepare for that point in my life in the future.

Help me to be wise and understanding about the changes in my life. Thank You for sending the Holy Spirit to give me patience and self-control and to bless my conversations with my parents. It's great to know I'm not alone in all of this. Amen.

Am I Normal?

Twelve-year-old Matt feels awkward because his eleven-year-old sister, Maddie, is taller than he is. Maddie doesn't like it either. She feels like a giant because she is taller than many of her friends. She doesn't like being the only girl in her class who wears a bra. It's hard to be patient during adolescence, but in a few years, Matt might be tall enough to be a basketball star, and Maddie might be no taller than she is now. They are both normal and have been all along.

Different Rates of Growth

Nearly everyone asks the question "Am I normal?" while they are growing up. Everyone's growth is controlled by a tiny organ called the **pituitary gland**. The pituitary gland is something like an automatic timer. It sends chemicals called hormones into the body. By producing these hormones, the pituitary gland affects many things in your body, including the way your body turns food into energy, your blood pressure, reproduction, and the growth of your sexual organs.

Each person's growth timer is set a little differently. You might begin the changes of adolescence anytime from nine years old until fourteen years old. In fact, there are some cases of people who begin even earlier or even later. The average girl will do her growing about two years before the average boy. There is so much variety among normal children, though, that a boy might enter adolescence before his twin sister.

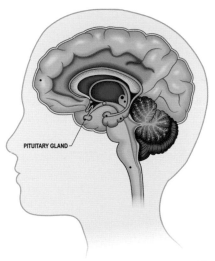

PITUITARY GLAND

Most people would rather do this extra growing at exactly the same time as their friends. Both early growers and late growers sometimes feel out of the ordinary during the time they are different from their friends. If this happens to you, try to be content with your own rate of growth. It is right for you. God planned it that way, because He knows what's best for you and your future!

Temporary Problems

Chances are, you look very different now than you did a year or two ago. It might be a little hard for you to get used to being so much taller and heavier than you were. Since hands and feet grow first, young people often feel awkward and out of proportion. Muscles don't usually develop as fast as bones do, so they end up trying to make an adult-size body work with child-size muscles. It might be hard, but the best thing you can do is laugh at these problems as you notice them in your body, remembering that they don't last long.

Many boys and girls worry about the weight they gain at this age. Others have the opposite problem. They get tall so fast, they don't grow sideways at all! But if they exercise and eat healthy food, they will end up being the size they are supposed to be.

Circumcision

You might have noticed something else that makes you different from some other boys. Some boys are circumcised soon after birth. A doctor cuts off the foreskin, a loose fold of skin covering the end of the penis.

In Bible times, God's people had their boy babies circumcised. This was a sign they belonged to God's special people. Joseph and Mary took Jesus to be circumcised when He was eight days old. Even today, most Jewish parents continue this custom. So do many parents who are not Jewish. They believe **circumcision** aids good health. It is easier to keep the penis clean when the foreskin is gone. It doesn't matter if you are circumcised or not. It does matter that you keep yourself clean and healthy.

Different Shapes and Sizes

Adolescent boys often worry about the size and shape of their testicles and penis. Girls often worry about the size and shape of their breasts. "Am

I normal?" they wonder. Normal people come in many different shapes and sizes. Even in the same person, one testicle (or one breast) may be bigger than the other.

Think how uninteresting life would be if everyone looked exactly alike! Instead, God has made each one of us special in some way. You may have something you don't like about yourself, but God has wonderfully designed you and has blessed you with unique abilities and gifts. There's so much more to you than just your appearance!

You can spend your life being unhappy about something you cannot change, or you can make the most of the good gifts God has given you. **The Holy Spirit will help you to appreciate God's blessings that make you who you are.** This is an exciting time in your life to develop the skills and talents that you will use as an adult. Enjoy working hard at the things you can change, like your abilities, but don't worry about the things you can't control, like the changes happening in your body. God's in control, and that's the way it's supposed to be!

God knows what your life will be like when you grow up. He is there to help you make the right choices, and He will be there and love you even when you make mistakes. God is with you to guide you. He placed you right where He wants you in His story; He has a plan for you to share His love with others.

And remember that Jesus was once your age and understands how you feel. Jesus experienced these same changes in His body! Remember God's promise, "I, the LORD, your God, hold your right hand; it is I who say to you, 'Fear not, I am the one who helps you'" (Isaiah 41:13).

> Do you not know that your body is a temple of the Holy Spirit within you, whom you have from God? You are not your own, for you were bought with a price. So glorify God in your body. (1 Corinthians 6:19–20)

Feeling Good about Your Sexuality

7

Jesus chose you to be His. What choices will you make as His child? You can choose between feeling good or bad about your body. You can choose between good things and bad things to put into your body. Think about how knowing you are a loved child of God, with the gift of a wonderful body created by your Father in heaven, makes a difference in the way you live.

You can choose TV shows, movies, books, websites, and magazines that give you good feelings about yourself and other people—or you can fill your mind and heart with unhealthy thoughts and ideas that are not God-pleasing and that do not respect God's perfect design for marriage and family. When you watch or buy things that are sinful, you are sharing and supporting that sin.

If you eat junk food, you are hurting your body. Your growing body will not get the nutrition it needs to be healthy, and you won't feel or look your best. If you watch or listen to "junk" or "garbage," you are hurting yourself spiritually, emotionally, and socially. You will hurt and weaken your faith.

You may feel like you're the only one who isn't watching "those" shows, or you may worry that your friends will make fun of you. But chances are, you aren't the only one of your friends who feels uncomfortable when someone in your group shows something inappropriate. Try to stay busy with activities that you know are not questionable. Suggest to your friends doing a different activity instead of watching an improper show or movie.

Sometimes, it may happen that you are the only one who is mature enough to understand that the group has made a bad choice. Then, some real courage is needed. "Be watchful, stand firm in the faith, act like men, be strong. Let all that you do be done in love" (1 Corinthians 16:13–14). Remember that there are other kids out there who feel just as you do. Your leadership may help your current friends to change. If not, maybe you need to find some new friends.

If kids make fun of you, they probably do not feel good about themselves either. Insecure and immature people often try to make themselves feel better by putting down someone else. Ignoring them is probably the best way to get them to stop teasing you. Bullies continue to do things because they know they've been successful in hurting you.

Many attractive, successful adults have felt just as you do when they were your age. Growing up can be very painful at times. If you take care of your body and listen only to what your heavenly Father says about you, you may feel more able to ignore other children who are hurtful.

The Holy Spirit is helping you to make good choices to keep your growing mind and your growing faith healthy. He will strengthen you. The Holy Spirit is also helping you to make good choices to keep your growing body healthy.

If you are a Christian, God's Spirit lives in your body. You are a valuable member of God's family. It matters what you put into your body. Remember, "you are not your own, for you were bought with a price. So glorify God in your body" (1 Corinthians 6:19–20).

Excessive use of alcohol and drug abuse do permanent damage to brain cells. Any use of alcohol and drugs interferes with your thinking and can cause you to make really bad choices that you might regret for a long time afterward.

Smoking can lead to serious problems, such as lung or oral cancer and heart disease. It also makes you less attractive. Smokers have bad breath, their clothes smell, and their teeth can become yellow. Using other tobacco products such as chewing tobacco is not safer. They, too, can cause gum disease and cancer. Smokeless tobacco irritates your gum tissue and can cause tooth decay, and it is even more addictive than cigarettes.

Another thing that can lead to serious problems is **pornography**. Pornography displays a human as a sex object, a thing to be used for someone else's pleasure. Some Internet sites, magazines, and X- and R-rated movies show the body as something to be used, abused, and lusted after rather than something to be thankful for, admired, and treated as a gift of God. You may hear that many or even all boys look at pornography and that it is something boys are supposed to do. But that is not true! Many boys your age and even much older have never looked at pornography. Because of the way God made boys' minds, pornography can seem very exciting to some, but that also means it can be very addictive, even at a young age. The best thing to do is to understand that this kind of material is out there and to do your best to not be exposed to it. It could harm your mind; your relationships with friends, girls, and your family; and how you relate to God for many years to come.

If you come across something that pops up on the Internet that doesn't seem like something you should be watching or something inappropriate that your friends suggest you see, don't even look. Pornography can become a harmful addiction, and it can affect your sexual health the rest of your life. Pornography is like poison for your mind.

Other people are affected by the choices you make about your body. If you smoke, the people who live in your home and who are around you will suffer the physical effects of secondhand smoke. For people who breathe in smoke that comes from the end of a cigarette, it can cause ear infections, lung or breathing problems, asthma attacks, or even cancer. A mother who smokes, drinks alcohol, or does drugs is much more likely to bear children who have serious physical and mental problems.

Those who abuse alcohol and drugs often cause accidents that harm others. As a preoccupation with alcohol and drugs takes control of them, they waste their lives, are unproductive, and destroy their relationships. Support of an illegal drug culture leads to many other terrible crimes.

Those who view pornography now are likely to affect their marriage later on. Pornography is "teaching" your body an unhealthy, selfish view of sex that does nothing to respect your future spouse. It only leads to emotional pain.

As the Holy Spirit works through God's Word, He gives us the power to honor God in the choices we make about what we put into our bodies and how we care for them. He helps us to live our life for Jesus—the one who lived, died, and now lives again for us!

Other people are affected by the choices you make with your body.

Not only what you do, but also what you say affects them too. If your friends are making bad decisions and saying inappropriate things, it's important to stop and think about other people's feelings before you get caught up in what your friends are doing.

God made you special, but remember that God created everyone else just right too. Everyone deserves to be respected as a child of God. You don't feel good when people tease you about the way you look or make you feel uncomfortable by talking about your body in a sexual way. Do not treat others that way or encourage others that do by laughing at or listening to such conversations.

You can be affected by other people's bad choices and sinful understanding of sex. If someone says things about your body that make you feel uncomfortable or if someone does or wants to do something to your body that you know is wrong, say no! Be sure to tell your parents, the school nurse, a favorite teacher, or your pastor. No one will get mad at you or feel any less of you.

Even if the person made you promise not to say anything, it's okay to tell "bad" secrets. If someone touches you in a way that doesn't feel right—or if a friend told you it happened to him or her—telling someone you trust is the best choice for everybody. Such behavior is inappropriate, and the person must be made to stop.

God doesn't want you to worry about what could happen, but it's smart to plan what you would do to get out of danger. Ask your parents about how to stay safe around strangers and how to deal with family members or acquaintances who act improperly. Remember that there are people you can trust and that God will always be there for you in any kind of trouble. He will help you to be braver and wiser than you ever thought you could be.

Sex is something God created as a blessing and delight to a husband and wife. *Unfortunately, people are sinful, and sin works to destroy any of God's blessings to us.* Contrary to what people in the world may tell us to do, it's not okay to go ahead and do whatever you want as long as it's fun and feels good. It's not okay to follow what everybody else is doing, even when you know it's wrong. It's not okay to use or abuse people by laughing at them or mocking them.

God has a better plan for you, His child. He wants you to love others enough to tell them when they are doing something wrong and harmful. With the Holy Spirit guiding and strengthening you, you can make God-pleasing decisions that respect others as children of God and that respect God's plan for healthy relationships and marriage.

> We are the temple of the living God; as God said, "I will make My dwelling among them and walk among them, and I will be their God, and they shall be My people." (2 Corinthians 6:16)

Lord, as I grow and change, help me to live as Your redeemed and sanctified child. You know what is best for me, and You want what is best for me. You gave me Your very best in Your Son, Jesus!

I need Your forgiveness when I am weak and Your enabling power to make me strong. Lead me to live as Your child. When I am tempted to act in ways that do not please You—in the way I dress, the words I say, the websites I search, the movies I watch, or the books I read—help me fight temptation and focus on whatever You would have me do. Keep before me the Good News that because Jesus died on the cross and "was raised from the dead by the glory of the Father, we too might walk in newness of life" (Romans 6:4). I know this new life in Christ is not the easy way, but I also know You will enable me to live through the power of the Holy Spirit.

When I'm unsure what this new life looks like or what I should do, point me to Your Word, which tells me that it is a life growing fruitfully in "love, joy, peace, patience, kindness, goodness, faithfulness, gentleness, self-control" (Galatians 5:22–23). Amen.

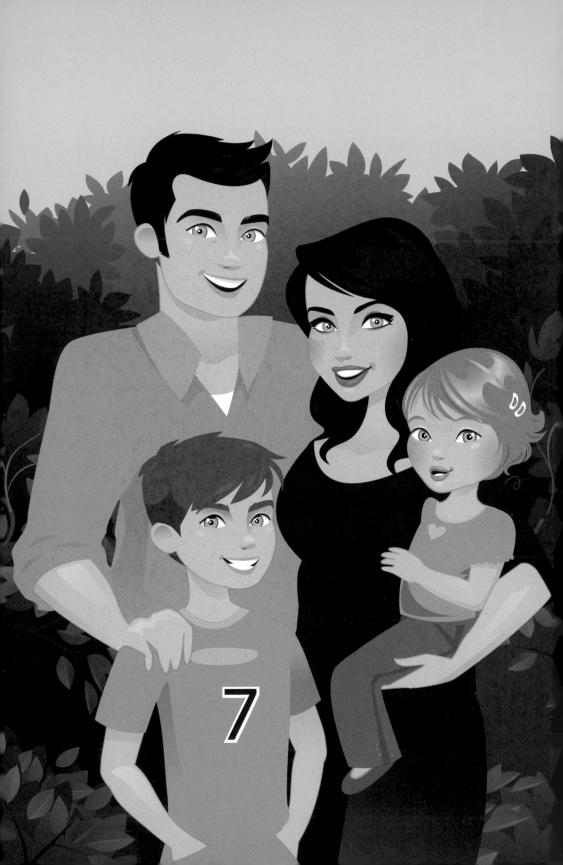

It's Great to Be Alive! 8

When God finished making the world, He looked at it and saw that it was good. He had made many, many different kinds of plants and animals. Each one was valuable in its own way.

God made each living thing able to bring new life into the world. Each is able to **reproduce** itself—to make more of its own kind.

Some flowers, for instance, reproduce when bees bring pollen (a yellow powder) from one flower to another. The pollen is like sperm cells. Seeds are formed when pollen joins the egg cells in the center of a flower.

A female fish lays many eggs in the water. The male fish swims over them and sprinkles them with sperm cells. New life begins wherever an egg and a sperm join.

Other animals reproduce very much as humans do. For instance, male dogs, elephants, and mice all have penises, which they use to place sperm inside the females.

But animals cannot love their mates in the way that humans do. They cannot have the same respect and care for each other. They can never have the joy humans find in a loving and caring marriage.

Animals often take very good care of their babies—for a while. Mother elephants take care of their babies for four years—much longer than most other animal mothers. But human babies need much more care, love, and teaching than any animal. They need parents who are able to make wise decisions, parents who can give them a good home for many years, parents who help them grow in the love and nurture of God's grace. (Read Deuteronomy 11:18–19.)

It takes a long time to grow up enough to be a good parent. Even for an adult, it's not an easy job. All parents make mistakes—sometimes serious ones.

It's a good thing that God has a special love for the people He made. What would we do if Jesus had not lived and died for us? Christian parents and children know that God forgives their mistakes for Jesus' sake. They know that God can and will help when trouble comes.

If you have children of your own someday, you will find great joy in loving and caring for them. You will have used God's good gift of sex to bring very special people into the world. By your love and care, you can show your children a little of what God's love is like.

God's love can make sex a wonderful part of your love for another person. Guided by Him, you can choose a wife who will share your life. The love you have for each other will be extra special if God lives in both of you.

That time seems a long way in the future, doesn't it? The growing years ahead of you are also God's gift—your time to get ready for adult life. You will learn to make good decisions, remembering that you are God's child. You can stay close to Jesus by reading and hearing about Him—and talking to Him in prayer. That way, you can grow in faith and in your faith life every day. You can discover good ways to use all the wonderful gifts He has given you.

God loves you more than you can even imagine! He wants you to be happy, and He wants to be with you forever. God designed this world with you in mind. He made everything else first, for your enjoyment, and then He made humans. We are the crown of His creation!

When you see your parents as a blessing from God to help take care of you and help you to grow to be your best, you can appreciate that gift. When you see your family members as blessings from God to support and encourage you, you can appreciate that gift. When you see God's will for respecting your body and others' as best for your happiness and health, you can appreciate that gift. When you see yourself as God's precious, loved, one-of-a-kind child, you can appreciate the gift of you! When you see that God gave you a purpose—to show love to others, you can feel satisfied and fulfilled.

Because of Jesus, you are a new creation—the old, sinful person has gone away and a new, Spirit-filled person is in its place. When you look at God's great plan for Your life and strive to follow His ways, you'll be able to say, "It's good to be alive!"

> *God saw everything that He had made, and behold, it was very good. (Genesis 1:31)*

Dear Father in heaven, I think I'm beginning to understand more and more about how You love me. But the more I realize how big You are and how small I am, I'm even more amazed that You know me so well and care about me so much. Sometimes, I don't feel very special.

But when I think that there are over seven billion people in the world, and You know my name and the number of hairs on my head, plus all my problems, my hopes and dreams, and my future, it's just amazing! "When I look at Your heavens, the work of Your fingers, the moon and the stars, which You have set in place, what is man that You are mindful of him, and the son of man that You care for him? Yet You have made him a little lower than the heavenly beings and crowned him with glory and honor. You have given him dominion over the works of Your hands" (Psalm 8:3–6).

Even though I sometimes don't like going through all of these changes, I am thankful that You are with me. I trust that You know what is best for me because You made me and because You designed our bodies just right. Guide me through Your Spirit to appreciate all these gifts You've given me and to take good care of them. Thank You for Your Son, who makes all things right when I mess up or when I am ungrateful. You are the one who can make me excited about my future—now and for eternity. Amen.

Some Words Used in This Book

acne (AK-nee) A condition in which the skin has many small spots called pimples, where the skin glands and hair follicles are swollen.

Adam's apple (ADD-ems APP-uhl) The name for the part of the front of the neck that sticks out. It is thyroid cartilage in the voice box, which enlarges in males at adolescence.

adolescence (a-doh-LES-sense) The years when a person changes from a child to an adult.

amniotic fluid (AM-ne-ot-ik FLOO-id) The fluid surrounding an unborn baby inside the uterus. The fluid acts as a shock absorber and thermostat (regulating temperature).

anus (AY-nuhs) The opening where bowel movements leave the body.

athletic supporter (ath-LEH-tik suh-PORT-er) Elastic underwear that holds the penis and testicles close to the body.

breast buds (brest budz) A slight elevation and enlargement of the nipple area.

Cesarean delivery (si-ZER-e-an de-LIV-er-ee) A surgical operation making an opening in the walls of the abdomen and uterus for the delivery of a baby.

characteristics (KAR-ik-tuh-RISS-tiks) The traits or qualities that make a person or thing special. A good singing voice, long legs, and brown eyes are characteristics a person might have.

circumcision (sur-kum-SIZH-un) A minor operation in which the loose skin, or foreskin, is removed from the end of the penis.

cramps (kramps) Mild to more intense pain caused by contracting uterus muscles that help push blood out during menstruation.

ejaculation (ee-JACK-yoo-LAY-shun) A discharge (coming out) of semen from the penis.

embryo (EM-bree-oh) The earliest stage in the development of an unborn baby; considered conception through the end of the eighth week.

emotions (ee-MOE-shuns) A mental reaction (such as happiness, affection, fear, or anger) shown by strong feeling and usually causing a physical effect.

erection (ee-RECK-shun) A time when the penis is stiff and stands out from the body.

estrogen (ES-treh-jen) A female hormone produced for the first time at puberty. Helps build strong bones and makes the lining of the uterus grow and thicken.

fallopian tube (fal-LOW-pee-an tube) The tube inside a woman's body that provides a passage for the egg cell from the ovary to the uterus.

feelings (FEE-ling) The state of your mind.

feminine (FEM-ih-nin) Something that is characteristic of women (the female gender). It refers to or describes something that women would have.

fetus (FEE-tuhs) An unborn baby in his or her mother's uterus, from two months after conception to birth.

fraternal twins (fruh-TUR-nul twins) Twins who grew from two different egg cells that were joined by two different sperm cells.

gender (JEN-der) The behavioral, cultural, or emotional traits typically associated with one sex.

gene (JEEN) A tiny part of a sperm cell or egg cell that carries characteristics from the father or the mother.

growing pains (GRO-ing paynz) Pains in the legs of children who are growing.

hormones (HOR-mones) Chemicals that control growth or other changes in the body.

identical twins (eye-DEN-ti-kul twins) Twins who grew from one egg cell that divided in two after it was joined by one sperm cell.

incubator (IN-kyoo-bay-ter) A glassed-in bed, specially equipped for babies who were born too soon and need extra care.

intercourse (IN-ter-kors) Also called sex. The act in which sperm cells leave a man's body and enter a woman's body. This happens when a man places his penis into a woman's vagina.

masculine (MAS-kyoo-lin) Something that is characteristic of men (the male gender). It refers to or describes something that men would have.

maxi pad (MAKS-ee pad) A soft pad used to catch the unneeded blood and tissue that flow from a woman's uterus during menstruation. See sanitary napkin.

menstruation (men-stroo-AY-shun) The monthly flow through the vagina of unneeded blood and tissue from the uterus. The beginning of the menstrual function is called menarche (MEN-are-kee).

nocturnal emission (noc-TER-nul ee-MISH-un) See wet dream.

organ (OR-gun) A part of the body that has a particular job to do.

ovary (OH-vuh-ree) The female organ in which egg cells develop and grow.

pantiliner (PAN-tee-li-ner) The smallest and thinnest maxi pads. See maxi pad.

penis (PEE-nihs) The male organ through which both urine and semen leave the body.

period (PEER-ee-ud) The regular monthly time during which a woman menstruates, usually three to seven days.

pituitary gland (pih-TYOO-ih-ter-ee gland) The tiny group of cells that makes hormones controlling body growth and the work of many organs in the body.

placenta (pluh-SEN-tuh) A special organ that develops on the wall of the uterus during pregnancy. The placenta helps food and oxygen move from the mother's bloodstream to the baby's bloodstream and carries wastes from the baby to the mother.

PMS (pee-em-es) Also called premenstrual syndrome. The period right before menstruation, which may be characterized by moodiness due to hormonal activity.

pornography (por-NOG-raf-ee) Literature, motion pictures, art, or other means of expression that, without any concern for personal or moral values, intend simply to be sexually arousing.

puberty (PYU-ber-tee) The state of first becoming able to reproduce sexually (create new life). This happens when sex hormones are produced and the sex organs mature. A visible sign of this is menstruation in girls and facial hair growth for boys.

pubic hair (PYOO-bick hair) The hair that, at puberty, appears on the sexual organs on the outside of the body (genitals).

pregnant (PREG-nuhnt) Carrying a growing baby in the uterus.

premature (pree-muh-TYOOR) Born too early, before the usual nine months of growing in the uterus has passed.

reproduce   (ree-proh-DOOS) To make more of the same kind.

reproductive organs (ree-proh-DUK-tiv OR-guns) The parts of the body used to create babies. In a boy, these include testicles, scrotum, and penis. In a girl, these include ovaries, fallopian tubes, uterus, vagina, and vulva.

sanitary napkin (SAN-ih-tair-ee NAP-kin) A soft pad used to catch the unneeded blood and tissues that flow from a woman's uterus during menstruation. See maxi pad.

scrotum   (SKROH-tuhm) The bag of skin in which the testicles hang between the legs of a male.

semen   (SEE-muhn) A milky liquid that has sperm cells in it.

sex   (SEKS) Male or female. Word used to identify the reproductive act. See intercourse.

sexual organs (SEKS-shoo-ul OR-guns) The body organs needed for reproduction, the creation of new life.

sonogram   (SAHN-o-gram) The visual image of an unborn baby inside the uterus made by sound waves during an ultrasound examination.

tampon   (TAM-pahn) A small piece of cloth (like cotton) that is placed into the vagina to catch the unneeded blood and tissue that flow from a woman's uterus during menstruation.

testicle   (TESS-ti-kuhl) The male organ in which sperm cells grow.

testosterone (tes-TAS-tehr-one) A male hormone that causes the development of the male reproductive system and sex characteristics.

uterus   (YOO-ter-us) The female organ inside which a baby grows.

vagina   (vuh-JY-nuh) A tunnel leading from the uterus to the outside of the body.

vulva   (VUL-vuh) The folds of skin and flesh that protect the opening to the vagina.

wet dream   A dream during which semen comes out of the penis.

womb   (WOOM) Uterus, the female organ inside which a baby grows.